Who Was
Nellie Bly?

by Margaret Gurevich

illustrated by Laurie A. Conley

Penguin Workshop

To Noah—don't let anything
stand in the way of your dreams—MG

For Pat, Jackie, and Paula, who inspire me
with their strength of spirit—LAC

PENGUIN WORKSHOP
An Imprint of Penguin Random House LLC, New York

Copyright © 2020 by Penguin Random House LLC. All rights reserved.
Published by Penguin Workshop, an imprint of Penguin Random House LLC, New York.
PENGUIN and PENGUIN WORKSHOP are trademarks of Penguin Books Ltd.
WHO HQ & Design is a registered trademark of Penguin Random House LLC.
Printed in the USA.

Visit us online at www.penguinrandomhouse.com.

Library of Congress Cataloging-in-Publication Data is available upon request.

ISBN 9781524787530 (paperback)   10 9 8 7 6 5 4 3
ISBN 9781524787547 (library binding)   10 9 8 7 6 5 4 3 2 1

Contents

Who Was Nellie Bly?

On January 25, 1890, a train rolled into Jersey City, New Jersey. Three timekeepers immediately stopped their watches. A large crowd applauded and cheered. Cannons fired. The crowd, however, was not there to see the train—but to greet the woman inside it.

"Nellie Bly!" the crowd cheered.

A sunburned woman walked off the train and tipped her hat to the adoring crowd. Her fans cheered louder.

After seventy-two days and twenty-two thousand miles, Nellie Bly had done what most believed was impossible—especially for a woman. She had traveled around the world. She was in a race against time to beat the "eighty days" in the title of a famous book published less than twenty years earlier: *Around the World in Eighty Days.* And Nellie had done it!

A ferry took Nellie to New York City. A carriage drove her across Newspaper Row—a street that was actually named Park Row, near city hall. It was called Newspaper Row because it was the home of the most important New York City newspapers. Crowds gathered and cheered and shouted her name as the carriage continued its drive to the *New York World*'s headquarters.

Even a rival publication, *The Cosmopolitan* magazine, sent Nellie roses to congratulate her. Nellie was amazed. Just three years earlier, she had no money. No one knew her name. The city's top papers would never have considered hiring her.

Now, she worked for the *New York World*, one of the most famous newspapers in the United States. Even newspapers in other countries published stories about Nellie Bly and her big trip around the world.

Just as she had always hoped, Nellie had become the "best-known and most widely talked-of young woman on Earth . . ."

CHAPTER 1
Early Years

Elizabeth Jane Cochran was born on May 5, 1864, in Pennsylvania. Her father, Michael, was a judge and landowner who founded the town of Cochran's Mills in the western part of the state. Both Michael and Elizabeth's mother, Mary Jane Kennedy, were widowed when they met. Michael had ten children with his first wife and five with Mary Jane. Elizabeth was their third child together.

Mary Jane wanted Elizabeth to stand out. Other children wore grays and browns. Mary Jane dressed Elizabeth in pink, frilly outfits. And because of this, people started calling Elizabeth, Pink.

When Elizabeth was only six years old, her father became sick and died. Even though Judge Cochran was wealthy, Elizabeth's mother was left with very little. This was because her father never made a will. A will is a legal document that explains who gets money and property in the case of someone's death. Without a will, Mary Jane had no rights to Judge Cochran's land or money. She had to figure out how to raise five children on her own.

Elizabeth quickly realized life was not easy for a single mother in the 1870s. Women usually had to depend on their husbands for money. When it came time to look for a husband herself, Elizabeth had a better plan. She instead looked for a career. She promised herself she would find a job to support both herself and her family. When she was fifteen, Elizabeth attended the Indiana Normal School in Indiana, Pennsylvania, to learn to become a teacher. Teaching was one of the few jobs women were allowed to have. But after only one semester, Elizabeth had to leave the school. Her mother didn't have the money to pay for her education.

Mary Jane decided to move her family to the city of Pittsburgh, where she thought she and her children might have more opportunities.

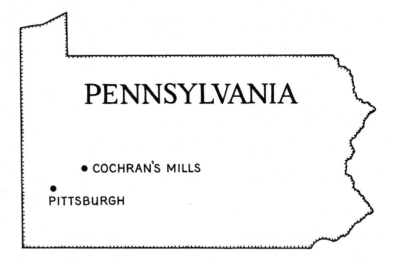

PENNSYLVANIA

• COCHRAN'S MILLS

•
PITTSBURGH

She bought a small house and made extra money by renting out rooms. Even though Elizabeth's older brothers were less educated than she was, they became clerks and managers at local businesses while she could find work only as a kitchen girl, tutor, housekeeper, or nanny.

None of those jobs involved her passion, though. Elizabeth's true passion was reading. Her favorite paper to read was the *Pittsburg Dispatch*.

Little did Elizabeth know that the *Dispatch* would lead her to the job of her dreams.

CHAPTER 2
Just a Normal Working Girl

At twenty years old, Elizabeth had been through many hardships. One morning, as she was reading the *Dispatch,* a column caught her eye. A man who called himself the "Quiet Observer" wrote that women should stay home and cook,

clean, and take care of their children. He felt that women who worked were not normal. Opinions like these were common in 1885, and they made Elizabeth angry. She had seen her mother struggle to take care of her children. She wanted to prove this "Quiet Observer" was wrong.

Elizabeth took out a sheet of paper and wrote a long letter to the editor. She said women should work if they wanted. They were just as smart and able as men. She signed her letter *Lonely Orphan Girl.*

George Madden, the managing editor of the *Pittsburg Dispatch*, was interested in finding out who the "Orphan Girl" was. He believed that the unknown letter writer could add spark to his newspaper, and he wanted to meet her. Unfortunately, Elizabeth had been too nervous to sign her name or include her address. George showed the letter to Erasmus Wilson, the man who secretly wrote as the "Quiet Observer." Erasmus had an idea. He told George to put an ad in the Letters to the Editor section asking the unknown "Orphan Girl" to send her name and address to the paper.

When Elizabeth saw George's ad, she got a great surprise. She didn't feel comfortable, however, replying with her personal information. Instead, the next morning, she marched directly to the *Dispatch*'s office.

Elizabeth's strong writing skills won over both George and Erasmus. To Elizabeth's delight, George hired her as a writer for the *Dispatch*.

But in the 1880s, it was considered "unladylike" for female reporters to write under their real names. Elizabeth needed to think of a pen name. George had heard someone in the office whistling "Nelly Bly," a popular song written by a famous composer named Stephen Foster. George loved that people already knew the name. He quickly wrote it down. Somehow, the name was accidentally spelled *Nellie* rather than *Nelly*. But from then on, Elizabeth would be known as Nellie Bly.

In 1885, female reporters were expected to write about fashion, shopping, or recipes. But Nellie wanted to write the same serious news stories as male reporters. She even took a job at a factory to experience the working conditions for herself. One of her earliest series of articles was about the daily lives of factory workers. Female readers wrote letters to the *Dispatch* praising Nellie for her work. They liked that she was writing about working women who were just like them.

Nellie told George she wanted to be a foreign reporter—someone who traveled and wrote articles for readers back home about their experiences. Nellie saw this as her chance to be taken seriously. She just needed to think of a place to go. Nellie remembered the railroad workers at her mother's boardinghouse talking about Mexico. They said you could travel there by train. Nellie ran to George with her idea, but he said the trip would be too dangerous. Nellie offered to take her mother so she wouldn't be alone. Finally, George agreed to pay for six months of travel through Mexico. Nellie and her mother were soon headed to Mexico City by train.

Nellie wrote about Mexico's wonderful food and polite people. But there were also things Nellie didn't like. Nellie thought the Mexican government treated its people unfairly. Other newspapers in the United States picked up the *Dispatch*'s stories, and word quickly got to Mexico. The Mexican government threatened to put her in jail. Because of this, Nellie and her mother had to cut their trip short and returned home after five months.

Back in Pittsburgh, George assigned Nellie to write for the women's page once again. For three months, Nellie argued with George about wanting to write more serious news stories. One day Nellie didn't show up for work. No one at the paper could find her. Finally, they realized that she had left a note for Erasmus Wilson. Over the years, he and Nellie had become friends. And Nellie didn't want to leave without saying goodbye to him.

The note said simply: "DEAR Q.O.—I am off for New York. Look out for me. BLY."

After three years at the *Dispatch*, Nellie was ready for her next adventure.

CHAPTER 3
New York Adventure

Nellie arrived in New York in May 1887. With well over a million people, New York City was the largest city in the United States. It was also the home of the most respected newspapers

in the country. One of those newspapers was the *New York World*, owned by Joseph Pulitzer. When he bought the paper in 1883, he made a lot of changes to both the *World* and journalism. He was the first to publish headlines in thick, bold type so they stood out. He added comics, illustrations, and articles on women's fashion and sports to the *New York World*.

Joseph Pulitzer had immigrated to America from Hungary in 1864. He fought for the Union Army during the Civil War. He hoped for a better world. Pulitzer said his paper would always fight for what was right. He created a newspaper that appealed to immigrants and the poor of New York City.

Joseph Pulitzer

Nellie set her sights on working for the *New York World*. She never forgot how much her family had struggled. Like Joseph Pulitzer, she wanted to do what was right and help others.

Nellie wrote Joseph and offered story ideas. He never wrote back. She wrote to other newspapers, but they didn't respond, either. Nellie needed to support both herself and her mother.

After four months of living in New York, Nellie was running out of money. And then one day, her purse was stolen! Nellie needed a job quickly.

She borrowed money for a cab from her landlady. Then, much as she'd done at the *Dispatch* two years before, she marched into the *New York World* offices. She asked the security guard to see the editor, Colonel John A. Cockerill. Nellie didn't have an appointment, but she had a great story idea.

THE WORLD

Nellie took an elevator to Colonel Cockerill's office. She shared many ideas. The editor said he had to talk to Joseph Pulitzer before assigning Nellie an article. He told Nellie to return on September 22. In the meantime, he gave

Colonel John A. Cockerill

her twenty-five dollars to make sure she didn't go to a rival paper with her ideas.

When they met again, Colonel Cockerill told Nellie he had the perfect assignment for her. Pulitzer had brought a new kind of journalism to his paper. He called it stunt reporting. It required journalists to go undercover to help them get the real details and facts of a story.

While most of today's newspapers frown on stunt reporting, it was very popular in the late 1800s. This undercover reporting style helped sell newspapers. It also presented opportunities for female writers to do much more serious reporting.

Female reporters were excited to move away from writing for the women's pages to instead cover important issues. They weren't afraid to go undercover to reveal the facts of a story.

The story that Cockerill and Pulitzer wanted Nellie to write was about Manhattan's Blackwell's Island, now called Roosevelt Island. Blackwell's Island, along with Ward's Island, was in the East

River along New York City. Both had prisons and asylums—hospitals for people with mental illness. In the 1800s, people who faced mental challenges suffered many harsh treatments presented as "therapy." There was often no hope for recovery. Doctors and family members sometimes gave up on those patients. They could easily be forgotten and remain in an asylum for the rest of their lives.

Manhattan's Blackwell's Island

Women Stunt Reporters

By 1900 in the United States, there were many more women reporters than there had been just twenty years earlier. They often used names other than their own when writing about topics that were considered unladylike at the time.

Annie Laurie

Annie Laurie (1863–1936), whose real name was Winifred Sweet Black Bonfils, reported for the *San Francisco Examiner*. She once pretended to faint on the streets of San Francisco to test how quickly local hospitals would respond. Because of her article, the city bought its first ambulance. She was also the only woman to report on the disastrous hurricane in Galveston, Texas, in 1900.

Eva Gay (1866–1956), whose real name was Eva McDonald Valesh, reported for the *St. Paul Globe*. As an undercover factory worker in 1888, she exposed a local garment factory's poor treatment of the women who

Eva Gay

worked there. Less than a month after her article was published, the women went on strike to protest

Nora Marks

the long hours, low pay, and dangerous working conditions.

Nora Marks (1863–1942), whose real name was Eleanor Stackhouse Atkinson, reported for the *Chicago Tribune*. She wrote about the poor treatment of children who had been accused of crimes. Some boys as young as ten were held at Chicago's Cook County Jail for more than a month.

The *World* had printed stories calling Ward's Island "disgracefully overcrowded." The *New York Times* had also written about poor conditions on Blackwell's Island. The *World* wanted to find proof.

Nellie's editor and publisher wanted her to find evidence at the Women's Lunatic Asylum on Blackwell's Island.

They told Nellie she would have to convince the staff she was mentally ill in order to get admitted into the hospital. No one had ever gone undercover as a patient in an asylum.

John Cockerill knew the risks Nellie would be taking if she agreed. "But if you can do it," he told her, "it's more than anyone would believe."

Nellie never turned down a challenge.

She agreed and prepared herself for what came next.

CHAPTER 4
Ten Days in a Madhouse

To prepare for her assignment, Nellie practiced expressions in front of a mirror. She wanted to make sure she looked like the other women in the asylum. She didn't comb her hair or brush her teeth. She roamed the streets of New York

looking lost. Her editor, Colonel Cockerill, hadn't given her much information, but she knew she could not go into the asylum as a reporter. She would be known as a patient named Nellie Brown.

Her first stop was the Temporary Home for Females, a boardinghouse for extremely poor women on Second Avenue, where she rented a room as Nellie Brown and avoided other women while trying to look sad and lonely. When it was time for bed, she said she was too scared to sleep. Nellie's acting worked! Her roommate even refused to share a room with her.

The next morning, Nellie would not stop crying about her missing things. Everyone at the boardinghouse knew she'd arrived empty-handed. The police took Nellie to the Essex Market Police Court. The judge at the court looked kind, and Nellie was worried he wouldn't send her to Blackwell's Island. She started crying again and said everyone's questions gave her a headache. The judge sent Nellie to Bellevue Hospital in Manhattan so the doctors could examine her.

Nellie told a doctor at Bellevue that she heard voices, and he recommended she go to Blackwell's Island. Nellie's plan had worked!

Nellie's time in the asylum was awful. She was forced to take ice-cold baths in dirty water and given used towels. At meal times, Nellie had to eat spoiled meat and moldy bread while the nurses ate fresh food! Nellie was always cold.

And she was scared. She came to realize that some women in the asylum shouldn't have been there. They had been admitted just because they were immigrants from another country, and the doctors who worked there didn't understand the language they were speaking! Nellie was worried she'd never get out.

Fortunately, a lawyer hired by the *New York World* came to get Nellie on October 4. She had been at the asylum for ten days, and she was glad to be free. But she also felt guilty leaving the other patients behind.

On October 9, 1887, the *World* published the first of two articles based on Nellie's experiences on Blackwell's Island. It was called "Behind Asylum Bars." Nellie's articles became so popular that her name was added to article headlines. Two months later, Nellie's book about her experiences, *Ten Days in a Mad-House*, was published.

The name Nellie Bly had become known in newspapers all over New York. More importantly, Nellie's story brought about positive changes to Blackwell's Island and other New York mental institutions.

CHAPTER 5
The Race Around the World

After the Blackwell's Island story, Nellie's dreams seemed to be coming true. Her job at the *New York World* paid for an apartment on New York's Upper West Side. Nellie and her mother could finally live comfortably. Nellie continued

writing the kinds of stories that made her famous—from revealing government wrongdoing to interviewing cowgirls. She also interviewed Belva Ann Lockwood, a woman who ran for president more than thirty years before women were even allowed to vote!

Belva Ann Lockwood

In 1888, Nellie's articles about her time in Mexico were turned into a book called *Six Months in Mexico*. A year later, Nellie's only novel, *The Mystery of Central Park*, was published. The novel got bad reviews, but Nellie wasn't upset. She continued writing exciting articles for the *World*.

Nellie's articles helped the *World* sell more papers than ever before. But it needed more stunts to *keep* people interested in their papers.

It found its next idea in *Around the World in Eighty Days*, a novel published in 1873 by a man named Jules Verne.

Around the World in Eighty Days tells the story of a man named Phileas Fogg who travels around the entire world in eighty days. When the book was first published, this kind of travel was just becoming possible. The first transcontinental railroad was built in the United States in 1869, making travel faster and easier. Before that, people traveled to the American West in wagons.

The Suez Canal opened in the Middle East that same year. The canal allowed people to sail directly between Europe and Asia without traveling around the continent of Africa. People who could afford to were eager to explore.

The opening of the Suez Canal, 1869

Jules Verne (1828–1905)

Jules Verne was a French author who is sometimes called the Father of Science Fiction. In his stories, characters use technology that hadn't yet been invented, and some inventions that actually came to exist in the future. Those included submarines powered by electricity, the helicopter, televisions, spacecraft, space shuttles, skywriting, and videophones (like early versions of FaceTime or Skype).

Some of his popular books are *20,000 Leagues Under the Sea*, *Journey to the Center of the Earth*, and *Around the World in Eighty Days*. His books were written in French and translated into more than 140 languages! They were also made into radio and television shows and movies.

The *New York World* wanted to send a reporter to travel around the world, like the character Phileas had. The editors wanted exciting news from foreign countries for their readers. And they knew making the trip in eighty days wouldn't be easy. A reporter could travel only by horse, train, or ship. Storms and bad weather could make all three impossible. Whoever made the trip would have to be up for the challenge.

For Nellie, this would be the stunt to end all stunts. But, in the 1800s, it wasn't considered safe or proper for women to travel alone. It was also assumed that a woman would need a lot of

luggage to hold her dresses. George W. Turner, the business manager of the *World*, did not want to send Nellie. "No one but a man can do this," he told her.

Nellie became angry. She'd proven herself over and over.

"Start the man," Nellie challenged, "and I'll start the same day for some other newspaper and beat him."

Nellie's editor, Colonel Cockerill, believed she would win. George didn't want another newspaper to scoop his story. The two men promised Nellie she could go.

On Monday, November 11, 1889, the colonel called Nellie into his office. He asked if she could leave on Thursday.

Nellie was determined. "I can start this minute," she told him.

Nellie knew she had to travel light to make all her connections quickly. She took only one dress and one jacket. And she packed what she felt was

 important: needles and thread, paper, underwear, her robe, slippers, and a drinking cup. Everything fit inside one small bag.

Bag packed, Nellie put on her lucky thumb ring. She'd been wearing it since her interview with the *World* two years ago. She also brought two self-winding watches. One was set to New York time, the other to wherever she'd be traveling.

There was one stop left. On Wednesday evening, she went to the *World* offices for her trip money and passport. Thursday morning, Nellie was ready. Her goal? To complete the trip in just seventy-five days.

CHAPTER 6
The Journey Begins

On November 14, 1889, Nellie boarded the steamship *Augusta Victoria* in Hoboken, New Jersey. It would sail across the Atlantic Ocean to England. This was Nellie's first time on a ship, and she became seasick.

As always, Nellie didn't let anything stop her. She got plenty of sleep and soon felt better. She was lucky to be traveling with a first-class ticket. Passengers in first class ate fancy meals, some with nine courses! In the evenings,

the ship held concerts out on the deck under the stars of the night sky. Although she enjoyed meeting some of the other passengers, all Nellie wanted to do was reach England and start her journey.

Almost one week after it set sail, the *Augusta Victoria* reached its first stop, London, England. The rough waters had put Nellie's ship behind schedule. She was sixteen hours late.

Tracy Greaves, the London reporter for the *World*, met Nellie as she was getting off the ship. He had exciting news. Jules Verne wanted to meet her! The catch? She had to be "willing to go without sleep or rest for two nights."

Nellie didn't mind. She and Tracy quickly boarded a carriage to the train station, where they caught a train to Southampton on the coast. There they boarded a boat and crossed the English Channel to continue their journey to Paris, France. In Paris, they boarded yet another train to the Vernes' home in Amiens.

A translator met with Tracy, Nellie, and Jules, and his wife, Honorine. The Vernes were happy to see Nellie, and she was excited to meet them. Before she left, Nellie asked to see Jules's study.

Jules wrote all his books there. Nellie expected something fancy, but the room had only a desk and window. A bottle of ink, one penholder, and a manuscript were the only things on the desk.

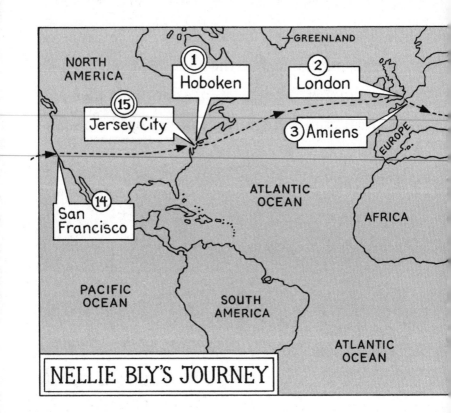

NELLIE BLY'S JOURNEY

As Nellie was leaving, Jules spoke to her in English for the first time. "Good luck, Nellie Bly," he told her.

Nellie was going to need it. With New Jersey, London, and France behind her, she had barely begun her journey. The stops ahead would include

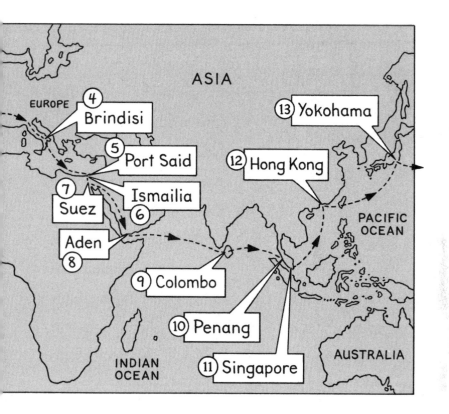

Brindisi (Italy), Port Said (Egypt), Ismailia (Egypt), Suez (Egypt), Aden (Yemen), Colombo (Southeast Asia), Penang (Malaysia), Singapore (Malaysia), Hong Kong (China), Yokohama (Japan), San Francisco, and then the return to Jersey City, New Jersey.

Nellie didn't know it, but another reporter was also trying to make a similar trip around the world. John Brisben Walker was the owner of *The Cosmopolitan* magazine. Like Joseph Pulitzer, he was interested in exciting stories that would boost sales of his magazine. When he read about Pulitzer's plan to send a reporter around the world, he decided to send someone on the same journey.

He asked his best reporter and editor, Elizabeth Bisland, to travel around the world—just like Nellie. But Nellie had headed east, leaving from North America and sailing to Europe. John Walker thought Elizabeth's journey would be quicker if she went west. Elizabeth left only a few hours after Nellie's ship had sailed from Hoboken.

Nellie Bly was in a race and she didn't even know it!

After leaving the Vernes, Nellie took a train to Italy. She hoped to see the Italian countryside. Unfortunately, it was too foggy, and the train's windows were

Elizabeth Bisland

dirty. Nellie was disappointed but focused on her task. Two hours later than planned, she finally boarded a ship called the *Victoria* sailing to Egypt.

Nellie sent a message to the offices of the *New York World* telling them she was fine but tired. She also said the journey was long and boring. The *World* wanted a report on Nellie's trip, but Nellie couldn't always find a telegraph office. Sometimes she had to send letters, which could take as long as two weeks to reach New York!

To keep readers interested, the *World* ran a contest. It asked readers to guess Nellie's arrival time. The person who came closest would win an all-expenses-paid trip to Europe. The *World* received almost a million entries during the course of Nellie's journey.

The Telegraph

The telegraph, perfected by Samuel F. B. Morse in 1844, was a messaging system that used coded electrical impulses—sent along wires—to transmit information. Operators would tap on a switch, using code to spell out the message. It was a revolutionary new style of communication that allowed people to contact one another over great distances. Messages that once took months to send could now be sent in minutes.

Telegraph systems were used mainly from the 1840s through the early part of the twentieth century.

Samuel F. B. Morse

Nellie went from Egypt on to Yemen. The other passengers complained about the heat, but not Nellie. She was just excited to learn about different people. In Yemen, she discovered that the people of Aden used wood to polish their teeth.

Nellie arrived in Colombo in Southeast Asia on December 8, two days ahead of schedule. She used the extra time to sightsee. She watched street magicians and a snake charmer.

Then she learned there would be a five-day delay. This would put Nellie three days behind schedule. Nellie called the delay an "outrage." Once again, she could think only about her journey and her deadline.

CHAPTER 7
Halfway There

Despite delays, Nellie's journey continued. She could tell her bad mood was making the other passengers uncomfortable, and she worked on taking things in stride. "Everything happens for the best," she told herself.

In Penang, she drank tea with monks in a temple. In Singapore, she rode a rickshaw and bought a monkey. Nellie insisted on traveling light, but she said her "willpower melted" when she saw the animal.

On day thirty-nine of her trip, two days earlier than planned, Nellie arrived in Hong Kong. The ship had picked up the days while at sea. Nellie admired the "castle-like" buildings around her. She was grateful her plan was back on track.

The ticket agent disagreed. "You are going to be beaten," he told Nellie.

Nellie knew he was wrong. She *was* behind schedule, she told the agent, but not anymore.

"Aren't you having a race around the world?" he asked her.

Nellie told the agent she was "running a race with Time." The ticket agent looked confused. He said he didn't know who Time was. He knew only about a woman named Elizabeth. She was racing around the world—just like Nellie. Nellie was surprised. She had no idea someone else was racing, too! But she decided it didn't matter. Her only job was to finish her own assignment.

"I promised my editor that I would go around the world in seventy-five days . . . ," she told the agent firmly. "If someone else wants to do the trip in less time, that is their concern."

Finishing on time wouldn't be easy. Nellie had to stay an extra five days in Hong Kong and spend Christmas in Canton, China. She hadn't seen her family in a long time, and she was homesick.

New Year's was more cheerful for Nellie. While on a ship to Japan, she and the other passengers drank champagne, ate oysters, and sang songs. Even Nellie's monkey, named McGinty, was on deck to ring in the New Year!

In Japan, Nellie and her companions were asked to take off their shoes before entering a house. Some of Nellie's fellow travelers did not want to follow this custom. They were given cloth slippers to put over their shoes instead. But Nellie didn't mind.

On January 7, Nellie's ship was to begin its journey from the city of Yokohama to California. The crew and the passengers wanted to wish her luck and show their support. The ship's chief engineer created a sign with Nellie's planned dock date in San Francisco. He hung it across the ship's engines in the engine room. Nellie loved the sign. It read:

FOR NELLIE BLY, WE'LL WIN OR DIE. JANUARY 20, 1890

As the ship neared San Francisco, Nellie only had three thousand miles of her trip left to go. She had traveled twenty-one thousand miles in sixty-eight days. She had a few delays, but she hadn't had to change her route. Still, the editors at the *World* were worried.

A snowstorm had begun. Snowdrifts were piling up, and the snow was heavy. It could take a week to clear the train tracks. Panicked,

her editors brainstormed alternate routes for Nellie to get from California to the East Coast.

On January 21, Nellie boarded a tugboat in San Francisco Bay. She tossed her bag behind her and carried McGinty. The boat sped to Oakland Mole, where Nellie received good news. Her friends in New York had found a route to avoid the snow blockade! Nellie boarded a special train the *World* arranged to carry her to Chicago.

Nellie could finally relax. She was almost home.

Nellie's US supporters cheered for her at each stop on the way to Chicago. They wanted to shake her hand. A man offered her a rabbit's foot for luck. Someone even asked her to run for governor of Kansas!

From Chicago, the train took Nellie off to Philadelphia, Pennsylvania. Nellie's mother, Mary Jane, was waiting there to surprise her. Nellie was sunburned and tired, but she was so happy to see her mother.

There was only a little piece of her journey left. On January 25, 1890, a train took Nellie from Philadelphia to Jersey City. The time was 3:51 p.m.

Nellie's trip around the world took seventy-two days, six hours, eleven minutes, and fourteen seconds. Nellie accomplished what no one had ever done before. Just as she had promised, Nellie had beat Time . . . and also her competitor in the race. Elizabeth Bisland had missed boarding one of her ships on time and so was delayed. She completed her trip around the world four days after Nellie.

CHAPTER 8
Trying Something New

Nellie's amazing race made her famous around the world. Companies rushed to promote their own products with Nellie's story and image. There was a Nellie Bly board game, Nellie Bly trading cards, and a Nellie Bly hat (like the one she wore on her travels). The *New York World* sold more papers than ever before. It even published her life story.

Nellie Bly board game

Nellie felt she deserved a raise. Joseph Pulitzer disagreed. He told Nellie her fame was reward enough. After the hard work of her trip around the world, Nellie felt Pulitzer didn't appreciate her—so she quit.

Nellie wasn't the only one who was angered by Joseph Pulitzer's actions. Even *The Journalist*, a publication that had poked fun at Nellie in the past, wrote about how she accomplished "what no other woman has been able to." It also criticized the way the *World* treated Nellie. Unfortunately, the article said, women's hard work is often dismissed, and they are not given the credit they deserve.

Nellie and her monkey now shared an apartment with her mother, her sister Kate, and Kate's daughter. Nellie supported them all. She needed to find work quickly. Her old friend Erasmus Wilson had no doubt Nellie would succeed. "She will just wait until a new idea strikes her, and go straightaway and carry it out," he said.

It turned out Nellie had a *few* new ideas. She earned $9,500 (about $277,000 today) to travel and give lectures about her trip. One of her

lectures was in Amiens, France, where she had interviewed Jules Verne. She also published a best-selling book about her trip. It was called *Nellie Bly's Book: Around the World in Seventy-Two Days*. Nellie also

signed a three-year contract with the publisher to write fiction for *New York Family Story Paper*, a weekly magazine. Nellie was to submit a story chapter each week. This was called serial fiction. People looked forward to reading each chapter of a book back then in the same way others look forward to their favorite television-show episodes today. Her salary was going to be $10,000 for the first year and $15,000 for each of the next two years. Nellie's old editor at the *World*, John

Cockerill, made $10,000 a year. He was one of the highest-paid newspaper editors in the country. At a time when the average salary for journalists was twenty to thirty-five dollars a week, Nellie's two-hundred-dollars-a-week salary was unheard of. Clearly, Nellie's new career seemed to make up for how poorly she was treated by her old newspaper.

The money from Nellie's job allowed her and her monkey to leave New York City to move in with her mother, who was living in a farmhouse in White Plains, New York.

Nellie was excited to write at home. After a lot of traveling, she wanted a break. But Nellie's new life wasn't easy. Writing fiction was harder than she thought it would be. Nellie couldn't come up with stories easily. Nellie's personal life was difficult, too. Her older brother Charles had died at twenty-eight years old, so Nellie helped take care of his wife and children. The responsibility was a lot for one person to handle. Nellie couldn't get used to all the changes and her new routine. Completing the terms of her contract had become more difficult for Nellie. She struggled to keep up with the stories she was assigned.

By 1893, Nellie's contract with the *New York*

Family Style Paper had ended. She missed being in the spotlight, and she needed to earn money. When the *New York World*'s new editor, Morrill Goddard, offered Nellie a job, she accepted. This time, she negotiated the kind of job that worked best for her—a columnist. Nellie returned to work on September 17, 1893. The *New York World*'s front-page headline shared the news. Big, bold letters said: "Nellie Bly Again."

Nellie's first story was about a woman named Emma Goldman, who was against government of any kind. Nellie was one of the first people to write Emma's side of the story.

Emma Goldman (1869–1940)

Emma Goldman was a political activist and author. She was known as an anarchist—someone who does not want any form of government to exist. She lectured on women's and workers' rights and social issues including equal education for all. Freedom of speech was also very important to her.

In 1906, Emma founded the journal *Mother Earth*, a monthly magazine that was published until 1917.

In July 1894, Nellie got another chance to show her skills as a serious journalist. Railroad workers had been on strike against the Pullman Palace Car Company for eight weeks. Centered in Chicago, workers rioted, raided, and damaged the company. They set buildings and trains on fire. People were afraid the railroad would go out of business. Nellie arrived in Chicago the last week of the strike. She was angry at the protesters for causing so much damage. But after speaking to the protesters and their families, she understood their side. She wrote about the struggles the workers faced and how their families didn't have enough money to buy food or pay rent. No other New York paper presented the workers' side of the story.

Although the story got Nellie the attention she wanted—and a job offer in 1895 at the *Chicago Times-Herald*—her career was still not what she was hoping for. Most of her assignments were not as serious as she would have liked. "I used to have such hopes," she wrote to her old friend Erasmus Wilson. After five weeks at the *Times-Herald*, Nellie needed a change.

She chose to leave journalism behind and try something new.

She decided to get married—to a millionaire.

CHAPTER 9
Married Life

Some people thought Nellie's marriage was another stunt assignment. She and Robert Seaman, a successful businessman, met at a dinner in a Chicago hotel and had known each other for only two weeks before they wed. Robert was seventy years old, and Nellie was thirty.

Robert's family wasn't

Robert Seaman

happy. They couldn't understand why such a young woman would want to marry a much older man. They thought Nellie may have only wanted Robert's money.

But Nellie had her own money and career. She never wanted to rely on a man. She didn't *need* to get married. She *wanted* to.

Nellie and Robert were married on April 5, 1895.

Nellie and Robert's early years together weren't easy. They moved into Robert's four-story townhouse in New York. Robert's brother and other family members lived there, too, and Nellie didn't get along with all of them. She started to see that Robert was a jealous man. He even had her followed.

One day, Nellie saw Robert's will and became very upset. He'd promised Nellie that he would take care of her and her mother. But he planned to leave them very little money. Even though Nellie didn't marry Robert for his money, she still felt hurt that he broke his promise to her. It also reminded Nellie of the promise she made to herself years ago—that she would never depend on anyone else.

In 1896, Arthur Brisbane had become the new editor of the *New York World*. He and Nellie had become friends when both worked for the paper. He asked her to come back to work. And Nellie was ready.

Arthur knew how talented Nellie was. Her first article was about the twenty-eighth National American Woman Suffrage convention in Washington, DC. The suffrage movement

focused on getting women the right to vote. Nellie interviewed Susan B. Anthony, one of the leaders of the movement, along with Elizabeth Cady Stanton.

In 1896, Robert decided to take Nellie and her family to Europe. This trip around the world would be more relaxing than Nellie's race had been. In August, she left her job at the *World* yet again. She was off on a more personal European adventure.

After Nellie's mother, younger sister, and niece returned to New York, Nellie and Robert lived in Europe for almost three years. Both Robert and Nellie thought Europe's doctors were better for Robert's failing health.

Just as they were preparing to return to New York in 1899, Nellie received some terrible news. Her sister Kate had died. Nellie was very upset. She wanted something new to distract her from her sorrow.

Susan B. Anthony and Elizabeth Cady Stanton

Susan B. Anthony and Elizabeth Cady Stanton were great friends and leaders of the woman suffrage movement. Both women were abolitionists—people who fought against slavery. Together they published the *Revolution*, a women's newspaper, from 1868–1870. In 1869, Elizabeth and Susan started the National Woman Suffrage Association (NWSA) and traveled all over the country to fight for women's rights, especially the right to vote. They also wanted women to have the same rights men did—like owning property and earning equal pay. Although Elizabeth died in 1902 and Susan in 1906, their hard work paid off when women finally got the right to vote in 1920.

Susan B. Anthony and Elizabeth Cady Stanton

Nellie became president of Robert's Iron Clad Manufacturing Company in Brooklyn. At that time, the company was $300,000 in debt. Nellie eventually paid back all the money that was owed, and the company once again became profitable.

In 1904, Robert died at home while reading the paper. His doctors thought he may have developed a heart condition because of a carriage accident he had a month earlier.

Iron Clad Manufacturing Company

Nellie focused on caring for her family. Her mother, her brothers and their wives, her late brother Charles's two teenagers, and Kate's daughter all lived in the townhouse with her. Nellie wanted her nieces and nephew to have the educational opportunities she never had.

Nellie also cared about the Iron Clad families. She did not want them to become dissatisfied like the Pullman workers she had interviewed years earlier. It was important that her employees be treated fairly. Nellie added showers, a dining room, gym, library with two librarians, and a bowling alley to the Iron Clad headquarters in Brooklyn. She also built a club room, complete with Ping-Pong and pool tables, games, and a piano. Nellie even added a hospital and charged factory workers just fifty cents for doctor visits. Most importantly, Nellie made sure the workers were paid a regular weekly salary.

Nellie loved the business world. Unfortunately, she wouldn't be managing her company for long. Some workers had stolen almost two million dollars from the business! It was 1911, and Nellie was bankrupt.

Nellie Bly: Businesswoman

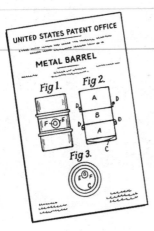

Nellie Bly was known for her writing and her reporting. But she was also a businesswoman. She invented a type of milk can as well as stacking garbage cans. By 1905, she had earned twenty-five patents for her inventions.

Nellie also started the American Steel Barrel Company. This was the first plant in the US to produce steel barrels. She even had business cards made up that said she was "the only woman in the world personally managing industries" of such a great size.

CHAPTER 10
War Correspondent

After Iron Clad failed, Nellie struggled financially, but Arthur Brisbane wanted to help. He was now the editor of the *New York Evening Journal*. His salary of more than $250,000 a year made him the highest-paid editor in the United States. He offered Nellie a job at the *New York Evening Journal*.

Once again Nellie was writing about women's rights. She also covered the Republican and Democratic political conventions of 1912. But Nellie was still worried about money. In 1914, she planned a trip to Austria to meet with someone who offered to buy the American Steel Barrel Company. Austria-Hungary declared war on Serbia on July 28, marking the start of World War I. That did not stop Nellie. She sailed on August 1, ready for whatever awaited her.

A large part of World War I was fought on the Eastern and Western Fronts. The Western Front fighting took place in France and Belgium.

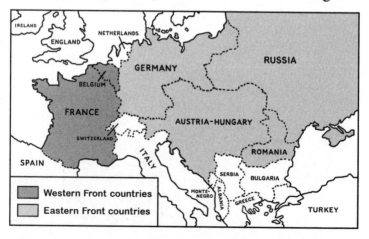

Fighting in the Eastern Front took place in Germany and Austria-Hungary on one side and Russia and Romania on the other side. Because she was already in Austria, Nellie sent a cable to Arthur Brisbane telling him she would send him three articles to start. She continued to send articles throughout the war. Nellie became the first woman to report from the Eastern Front.

She was a brave reporter who even hid in a trench during an attack. She visited soldiers in hospitals so that she could report on their suffering firsthand.

World War I (1914–1918)

World War I started in July 1914 between Austria and Serbia.

Eventually, the war was fought by many countries that took sides between the Central Powers and the Allied Powers. The Central Powers included Austria-Hungary, Germany, Bulgaria, and the Ottoman Empire. The Allied Powers included Serbia, Russia, France, the United Kingdom, Italy, Belgium, and the United States.

World War I ended on November 11, 1918, when both sides signed an agreement to end the war. The agreement was called an armistice. World War I was called the Great War because it was a global war fought in Europe, Africa, the Middle East, Pacific Islands, and China. It was the first war where tanks and planes were used in fighting. No one thought there would be another war like it again. But there was.

By the end of World War II in 1945, historians began calling the Great War simply the First World War.

CHAPTER 11
The Best Reporter in America

Nellie returned to New York in 1919 and continued writing for the *New York Evening Journal*. She was paid $100 a week. This was half her salary of twenty years before, but Nellie was thankful she had a job.

She wrote about important topics like homelessness and used her column to help out-of-work mothers find jobs. One of her biggest causes was trying to help children, especially orphans, find families to provide homes for them. She even sometimes took children into her home while she searched for people to adopt them.

Nellie's mother died on February 26, 1921. Nellie herself often complained about being

tired and weak. She developed a lung infection and died on January 27, 1922. She was fifty-seven years old.

Her longtime friend Arthur Brisbane wrote a long column in the *New York Evening Journal*. He called Nellie "the best reporter in America."

NEW YORK TIMES,

NELLIE BLY, JOURNALIST, DIES OF PNEUMONIA

Famous for Rapid Trip Around the World in 1889 and Other Daring Exploits.

The *New York World*'s obituary—a news article that reports a person's death—listed Nellie's biggest stories.

Throughout her life, Nellie used her voice and words to fight for people who had no one to listen to them. Her daring attitude opened the doors for female journalists throughout the United States and beyond. By the time Nellie died, female reporters were becoming more common in the newsroom. Nellie's words also pushed people in power to do the right thing. Nellie's name is now known all around the world.

In 2019, the city of New York announced that it would create a public statue of this daring female reporter. Her legacy lives on in the place where she took on one of her most challenging assignments. There will be a permanent Nellie Bly monument built on Roosevelt Island, once called Blackwell's Island. The statue of Nellie will help ensure that the spirit of this brave journalist will never be forgotten.

Timeline of Nellie Bly's Life

1864	Born Elizabeth Jane Cochran on May 5 in Cochran's Mills, Pennsylvania
1885	Begins working for *Pittsburg Dispatch*, under the name Nellie Bly
1886	Works as foreign reporter in Mexico
1887	Completes undercover assignment for *New York World* at Blackwell's Island
	Ten Days in a Mad-House is published
1889	Begins trip around the world on November 14
1890	Completes her trip around the world
1894	Covers the Pullman Palace Car Company strike, becoming only reporter to show the strikers' side
1895	Leaves *Chicago Times-Herald* to marry Robert Seaman
1896	Rejoins *New York World*
	Interviews Susan B. Anthony
1899	Becomes president of Iron Clad Manufacturing Company
1904	Husband, Robert Seaman, dies
1912	Gets job at *New York Evening Journal*
1914	Becomes the first woman to report from the Eastern Front during World War I
1922	Dies on January 27 in New York City

Timeline of the World

1865	—	President Abraham Lincoln is assassinated
1866	—	The American Society for the Prevention of Cruelty to Animals (ASPCA) is founded
1869	—	Wyoming is the first territory to grant women the right to vote
1873	—	*Around the World in Eighty Days* by Jules Verne is published
1876	—	Alexander Graham Bell invents the telephone
1879	—	Thomas Alva Edison invents the lightbulb
1883	—	The Brooklyn Bridge opens
1898	—	The US battleship *Maine* is sunk in Havana harbor
1903	—	First narrative silent movie, *The Great Train Robbery*, is made
1905	—	First movie theater in the world opens in Pittsburgh, Pennsylvania
1911	—	Marie Curie wins Nobel Prize in chemistry, becoming the first person to win two Nobel Prizes
1912	—	The *Titanic* sinks after hitting an iceberg
1914	—	World War I begins in Europe
1921	—	Congresswoman Alice Mary Robertson becomes the first woman to preside over the floor of US House of Representatives
1922	—	Construction begins on Yankee Stadium in New York City

Bibliography

*Books for young readers

*Bankston, John. ***Nellie Bly: Journalist.*** New York: Chelsea House, 2011.

*Castaldo, Nancy. ***The Race Around the World.*** New York: Random House, 2015.

"8 Jules Verne Inventions That Came True (Pictures)." ***National Geographic,*** February 8, 2011. https://news.nationalgeographic.com/news/2011/02/pictures/110208-jules-verne-google-doodle-183rd-birthday-anniversary/.

Fowler, Dave. "Titanic Survivors." ***Titanic Facts.*** Accessed February 18, 2020. https://titanicfacts.net/titanic-survivors/.

*Fredeen, Charles. ***Nellie Bly: Daredevil Reporter.*** Minneapolis, MN: Lerner Publications, 2000.

Goodman, Matthew. ***Eighty Days: Nellie Bly and Elizabeth Bisland's History-Making Race Around the World.*** New York: Ballantine Books, 2013.

*Kendall, Martha E. ***Nellie Bly: Reporter for the World.*** Brookfield, CT: The Millbrook Press, 1992.

*Krensky, Stephen. ***Nellie Bly: A Name to be Reckoned With.*** New York: Aladdin Paperbacks, 2003.

*Kroeger, Brooke. ***Nellie Bly: Daredevil, Reporter, Feminist.*** New York: Times Books, 1994.

McClurg, Jocelyn. "Serial Novels Were the Craze in the 19th Century." *Hartford Courant,* September 11, 1994. http://articles.courant. com/1994-09-11/news/9409110110_1_serial-novels-installment.

Ming, Yi, trans. "The Japanese Custom of Removing Shoes." *Vision Times,* December 2, 2016. http://www.visiontimes.com/2016/12/02/ the-japanese-custom-of-removing-shoes.html.

Noyes, Deborah. *Ten Days a Madwoman: The Daring Times and Turbulent Life of the Original "Girl" Reporter, Nellie Bly*. New York: Viking, 2016.

PBS. "Yellow Journalism." *Crucible of Empire: The Spanish-American War.* Accessed February 18, 2020. https://www.pbs.org/crucible/ frames/_journalism.html.

South Carolina ETV Commission. "Telegraph and Telephone | Kids Work!" *Knowitall.org.* Accessed February 18, 2020. https://knowitall.org/ document/telegraph-and-telephone-kids-work.

Todd, Kim. "These Women Reporters Went Undercover to Get the Most Important Scoops of Their Day." *Smithsonian Magazine*, November 2016. https://www.smithsonianmag.com/history/women- reporters-undercover-most-important-scoops-day-180960775/.

Treasure, Novel. "Is Morse Code Used Today?—The Brief History and Importance of Morse Code." *Owlcation.* Last modified February 18, 2020. https://owlcation.com/humanities/morse_code.

"World War 1 Facts." *National Geographic Kids.* Accessed February 18, 2020. https://www.natgeokids.com/uk/discover/history/ generalhistory/first-world-war/.